Introduction

National 5 French

The course specifications for National 5 French changed in 2017 and Units and Unit Assessments were removed. The only change to the exam papers, however, was the removal of 'overall purpose' questions for Reading and Listening. The 2017 and 2018 Past Papers reflect this, and the 2016 paper remains an incredibly useful revision tool. The questions contained in this book of Past Papers provide excellent representative exam practice. Using them as part of your revision will help you to learn the vital skills and techniques needed for the written exam, and will help you to identify any knowledge gaps you may have, prior to the exam season in May–June.

The course

The National 5 French course aims to enable you to develop the ability to read, listen, talk and write in French, that is to understand and use French, and to apply your knowledge and understanding of the language. The course offers the opportunity to develop detailed language skills in the real-life contexts of society, learning, employability and culture.

How the course is graded

The Course assessment will take the form of a performance, a writing assignment and a written exam.

The performance will be a presentation and discussion with your teacher, which will be recorded and marked by your teacher. It is worth 25% of your final mark.

The topic for the writing assignment will be agreed between you and your teacher. It will be carried out in class, under supervised conditions. It is worth 12.5% of your final mark.

This book will help you practise for the *written exam* you will sit in May.

The exams

Reading and Writing

- exam time: 1 hour 30 minutes
- total marks: 50
- weighting in final grade: 37.5%

What you have to do

- Read three passages of just under 200 words each, and answer questions about them in English.
- write 120–200 words in French in the form of an email, applying for a job or work placement: there will be six bullet points for you to address.

Listening

- exam time: 25 minutes
- total marks: 20
- weighting in final grade: 25%

What you have to do

- part 1: listen to a monologue in French, and answer questions in English
- part 2: listen to a dialogue In French, and answer questions about it in English.

How to improve your mark!

Every year, examiners notice the same kind of mistakes being made, and also they regularly come across some excellent work. They give advice in the three key areas of reading, listening and writing to help students do better. Here are some key points from their advice.

Reading

Make sure that your answers include detail in Reading. Remember, an answer of only one word will not normally be enough to gain a mark. However, you do not have to answer in sentences; bullet points are fine. Pick out detail from longer chunks of language, rather than focusing on individual words. Read the whole message, then pick out the key points, using the questions as a guide as to where to look. Detailed answers are generally required, so pay particular attention to words like *assez, très, trop, vraiment* and to negatives. Make sure you get the details of numbers, day, times, etc. right.

Take care when using dictionaries where a word has more than one meaning. Learn to choose the correct meaning from a list of meanings in a dictionary.

Beware of *faux amis*: *journée* means day, not journey, *travailler* means work, not travel, for instance!

In responding to the questions in the Reading papers, you should be guided by the number of points awarded for each question. You should give as much detail in your answer as you have understood but should not put down everything which is in the original text, as you are wasting time. The question itself usually indicates the amount of information required by stating in bold, e.g. "State **two** things" or "Give **any two**". If the question says "state any two things", it means that there are more than two possibilities. Just choose the two you are happiest with and stick to them. Only give alternatives if you are absolutely unsure of what is correct.

If you have time at the end, you should re-read your answers to make sure that they make sense and that your English expression is as good as it can be.

Listening

This is the paper that improves most with practice. So use the Listening papers in this book several times, to get used to the format of the exam.

Not giving enough detail is still a major reason for candidates losing marks. Many answers are correct as far as they go but were not sufficiently detailed to score marks. The same rules as for Reading apply.

You hear each of the Listening texts three times, so make use of the third listening to check the accuracy and specific details of your answers.

Be sure you are able to give accurate answers through confident knowledge of numbers, common adjectives, weather expressions, prepositions and question words, so that some of the "easier" points of information are not lost through lack of sufficiently accurate details.

In responding to the questions in the Listening papers, you should be guided by the number of points awarded for each question, and by the wording of the question. You should give as much detail in your answer as you have understood but should not write down everything you hear. The question itself usually indicates the amount of information required by stating in bold, e.g. "State **two** of them".

Make sure you put a line through any notes you have made.

Writing

This, along with Talking, is where students do best. It is a chance for you to know what your answers to the first four bullet points are in advance. Make sure you have some good material prepared and learned, ready to use in the exam.

Also, where learners write pieces that are too lengthy, this certainly does not help their performance. So stick to the 20–30 words per bullet point.

The examiners say many of the pieces are vibrant and refreshing in terms of style and content. At the upper level, the majority of candidates write well, and the range of language used is impressive. So look at the success criteria in the Answer section and try to model your writing on it. This applies particularly to the last two bullet points. Practise writing answers to the final two bullet points, which are different in every exam, adapting material you already know rather than using a dictionary to translate ideas from English.

You should ensure that you are careful when you read the information regarding the job you are applying for, and make sure your answer is tailored to fit that. Depending on the job, you may have to alter your strengths or the experience you are claiming. You should prepare in French a description of some "soft" skills that

are transferable, for instance, working with the public, able to communicate, good at working as part of a team or with others.

You should avoid writing long lists of things such as school subjects (and then repeating the list with a past or future verb tense) as part of your answers.

Use the dictionary to check the accuracy of what you have written (spelling, accents, genders, etc.) but not to create new sentences, particularly when dealing with the last two bullet points. You should have everything you need prepared when you come into the exam.

Be aware of the extended criteria to be used in assessing performances in Writing, so that you know what is required in terms of content, accuracy and range and variety of language to achieve the good and very good categories. Ensure that your handwriting is legible (particularly when writing in French) and distinguish clearly between rough notes and what you wish to be considered as final answers. Make sure you score out your notes!

You should bear the following points in mind:

- there are six bullet points to answer: the first four are always the same, the last two vary from year to year

- each of the first four bullet points should have between 25 and 30 words to address it properly

- answering the first four bullet points correctly will get you 12/20. Each of the last two, if answered correctly, will get an additional 4 marks

- you should aim to write about 20 words for each of these last two points, but do not try to write too much, as this might mean you are more likely to get things wrong

- you will be assessed on how well you have answered the points, and on the accuracy of your language

- you should also try to have a variety of tenses in your preparation for the first four bullet points, including past, future and conditional if you can

- for a mark of good or very good, you should have some complex language, such as longer, varied sentences and conjunctions, so have some sub-clauses ready, starting with words like "et", "ou", "mais", "parce que", "quand", etc.

Good luck!

Remember that the rewards for passing National 5 French are well worth it! Your pass will help you get the future you want for yourself. In the exam, be confident in your own ability. If you're not sure how to answer a question, trust your instincts and just give it a go anyway – keep calm and don't panic! GOOD LUCK!

Study Skills – what you need to know to pass exams!

General exam revision: 20 top tips

When preparing for exams, it is easy to feel unsure of where to start or how to revise. This guide to general exam revision provides a good starting place, and, as these are very general tips, they can be applied to all your exams.

1. Start revising in good time.

Don't leave revision until the last minute – this will make you panic and it will be difficult to learn. Make a revision timetable that counts down the weeks to go.

2. Work to a study plan.

Set up sessions of work spread through the weeks ahead. Make sure each session has a focus and a clear purpose. What will you study, when and why? Be realistic about what you can achieve in each session, and don't be afraid to adjust your plans as needed.

3. Make sure you know exactly when your exams are.

Get your exam dates from the SQA website and use the timetable builder tool to create your own exam schedule. You will also get a personalised timetable from your school, but this might not be until close to the exam period.

4. Make sure that you know the topics that make up each course.

Studying is easier if material is in manageable chunks – why not use the SQA topic headings or create your own from your class notes? Ask your teacher for help on this if you are not sure.

5. Break the chunks up into even smaller bits.

The small chunks should be easier to cope with. Remember that they fit together to make larger ideas. Even the process of chunking down will help!

6. Ask yourself these key questions for each course:

- Are all topics compulsory or are there choices?
- Which topics seem to come up time and time again?
- Which topics are your strongest and which are your weakest?

Use your answers to these questions to work out how much time you will need to spend revising each topic.

7. Make sure you know what to expect in the exam.

The subject-specific introduction to this book will help with this. Make sure you can answer these questions:

- How is the paper structured?
- How much time is there for each part of the exam?
- What types of question are involved? These will vary depending on the subject so read the subject-specific section carefully.

8. Past papers are a vital revision tool!

Use past papers to support your revision wherever possible. This book contains the answers and mark schemes too – refer to these carefully when checking your work. Using the mark scheme is useful; even if you don't manage to get all the marks available first time when you first practise, it helps you identify how to extend and develop your answers to get more marks next time – and of course, in the real exam.

9. Use study methods that work well for you.

People study and learn in different ways. Reading and looking at diagrams suits some students. Others prefer to listen and hear material – what about reading out loud or getting a friend or family member to do this for you? You could also record and play back material.

10. There are three tried and tested ways to make material stick in your long-term memory:

- Practising – e.g. rehearsal, repeating
- Organising – e.g. making drawings, lists, diagrams, tables, memory aids
- Elaborating – e.g. incorporating the material into a story or an imagined journey

11. Learn actively.

Most people prefer to learn actively – for example, making notes, highlighting, redrawing and redrafting, making up memory aids, or writing past paper answers. A good way to stay engaged and inspired is to mix and match these methods – find the combination that best suits you. This is likely to vary depending on the topic or subject.

12. Be an expert.

Be sure to have a few areas in which you feel you are an expert. This often works because at least some of them will come up, which can boost confidence.

13. Try some visual methods.

Use symbols, diagrams, charts, flashcards, post-it notes etc. Don't forget – the brain takes in chunked images more easily than loads of text.

14. Remember – practice makes perfect.

Work on difficult areas again and again. Look and read – then test yourself. You cannot do this too much.

15. Try past papers against the clock.

Practise writing answers in a set time. This is a good habit from the start but is especially important when you get closer to exam time.

16. Collaborate with friends.

Test each other and talk about the material – this can really help. Two brains are better than one! It is amazing how talking about a problem can help you solve it.

17. Know your weaknesses.

Ask your teacher for help to identify what you don't know. Try to do this as early as possible. If you are having trouble, it is probably with a difficult topic, so your teacher will already be aware of this – most students will find it tough.

18. Have your materials organised and ready.

Know what is needed for each exam:

- Do you need a calculator or a ruler?
- Should you have pencils as well as pens?
- Will you need water or paper tissues?

19. Make full use of school resources.

Find out what support is on offer:

- Are there study classes available?
- When is the library open?
- When is the best time to ask for extra help?
- Can you borrow textbooks, study guides, past papers, etc.?
- Is school open for Easter revision?

20. Keep fit and healthy!

Try to stick to a routine as much as possible, including with sleep. If you are tired, sluggish or dehydrated, it is difficult to see how concentration is even possible. Combine study with relaxation, drink plenty of water, eat sensibly, and get fresh air and exercise – all these things will help more than you could imagine. Good luck!

NATIONAL 5

2016

N5

National Qualifications 2016

Mark

X730/75/01

French Reading

MONDAY, 16 MAY
1:00 PM – 2:30 PM

Fill in these boxes and read what is printed below.

Full name of centre

Town

Forename(s)

Surname

Number of seat

Date of birth

Day   Month   Year   Scottish candidate number

Total marks — 30

Attempt ALL questions.

Write your answers clearly, in **English**, in the spaces provided in this booklet.

You may use a French dictionary.

Additional space for answers is provided at the end of this booklet. If you use this space you must clearly identify the question number you are attempting.

Use **blue** or **black** ink.

There is a separate question and answer booklet for Writing. You must complete your answer for Writing in the question and answer booklet for Writing.

Before leaving the examination room you must give both booklets to the Invigilator; if you do not, you may lose all the marks for this paper.

MARKS | DO NOT WRITE IN THIS MARGIN

Total marks — 30

Attempt ALL questions

Text 1

You read the following article about Paris Plage, a beach in the centre of Paris.

Chaque été depuis treize ans, un coin de Paris se transforme en plage de sable fin sur la rive droite de la Seine*.

C'est vraiment un lieu pour tout le monde: par exemple, les enfants peuvent participer aux concours des châteaux de sable ou faire voler des cerfs-volants et les adultes peuvent tout simplement se détendre au soleil en lisant un livre.

Il y a un écran géant en face de la plage pour ceux qui ne veulent pas rater les événements sportifs de l'été.

Olivier, 18 ans, est grand fan de la plage de la capitale. Il dit, «C'est génial pour les jeunes parisiens parce qu'il y en a beaucoup qui n'ont pas la possibilité d'aller au bord de la mer. Ils peuvent aller à cette plage sans quitter Paris. L'année dernière, j'y suis allé chaque après-midi pendant les grandes vacances. C'était un bon point de rencontre pour moi et mes amis et c'était gratuit!»

Farid n'est pas d'accord. «Paris Plage n'est pas une vraie plage car on n'a même pas le droit de se baigner. Je préférerais aller à une station balnéaire ou à une piscine en plein air.»

la Seine* – the name of the river in Paris

Questions

(a) Complete the sentence.　　　　1

There has been a beach in Paris every summer for

_____.

(b) The beach has something for everyone.

　(i) What is there for children? State **two** things.　　　　2

_____

_____

MARKS | DO NOT WRITE IN THIS MARGIN

Text 1 Questions (continued)

(b) (continued)

    (ii) What can adults do there? State any **one** thing.   **1**

_____

_____

(c) There is also a giant screen. Who can benefit from this?   **1**

_____

_____

(d) Olivier thinks that the beach is great for young Parisians. Why?   **2**

_____

_____

(e) Olivier went to the beach every afternoon last year. What does he say about it? State any **one** thing.   **1**

_____

_____

(f) Farid says Paris Plage is not a real beach.

    (i) Why does he think this?   **1**

_____

_____

    (ii) What would he prefer to do? State any **one** thing.   **1**

_____

[Turn over

MARKS | DO NOT WRITE IN THIS MARGIN

Text 2

You read an article about life in the city and in the countryside.

De nos jours il y a beaucoup de gens qui cherchent à vivre à la campagne. Ils veulent passer plus de temps à l'extérieur et se sentir plus en sécurité.

Mais est-ce que cette vie est vraiment meilleure que la vie en ville?

Voici un témoignage de Cécile qui a vécu les deux vies.

«Je viens d'un petit village mais je n'aimais pas y vivre. Il n'y avait rien à faire pour les jeunes, donc je m'ennuyais beaucoup.

Donc à l'âge de 17 ans je suis partie pour trouver du travail en ville. J'ai toute de suite adoré la vie en ville. J'aimais le fait que personne ne me connaissait et qu'il y avait un choix de divertissements. Mais après quelques années, j'ai changé d'avis. La circulation commençait à m'énerver et j'étais toujours pressée.

J'ai donc décidé d'acheter une maison secondaire à la campagne et je ne le regrette pas. J'ai deux chiens qui adorent courir dans les champs et je peux oublier tous les soucis de la vie quotidienne.

Personnellement je crois que ma situation est idéale car je mène une vie équilibrée. Je profite de l'animation de la ville et de la tranquillité de la campagne.»

Questions

(a) Why do many people want to live in the countryside? State **two** things.　　2

_____

_____

(b) What does Cécile say about the small village where she lived? Tick (✓) the correct statement.　　1

Everyone knew everyone.	
She was really bored.	
There were not many young people.	

MARKS

Text 2 Questions (continued)

(c) Cécile moved to the city when she was 17. What did she like about city life at first? State **two** things.

2

_____

_____

(d) In what ways did her opinion of city life change after a few years? State any **one** thing.

1

_____

_____

(e) She has no regrets about having bought a house in the country. Why? State **two** things.

2

_____

_____

(f) Why does she think she has a good balance in her life now? State **two** things.

2

_____

_____

[Turn over

MARKS | DO NOT WRITE IN THIS MARGIN

Text 3

You read an article where a student, Michel, talks about work experience.

Je suis étudiant à la faculté de droit et comme la plupart des étudiants j'ai fait un stage en entreprise chaque été. C'est un moyen d'avoir de l'expérience pratique et de gagner un peu d'argent.

Cependant, trouver un bon stage n'est pas toujours facile. On a une chance sur deux de tomber sur un stage "perte-de-temps". Dans certaines entreprises on a trop de responsabilités tandis que dans d'autres on sert le café, c'est tout. En même temps, quand on est stagiaire*, il est parfois difficile de gérer de nouvelles tâches.

Moi, j'ai fait deux stages bien différents. Le premier était épuisant et en plus, le patron était toujours de mauvaise humeur et j'avais peur de poser des questions si j'avais un problème. Par contre, le deuxième stage était une expérience positive. J'ai appris énormément de choses, j'ai assisté aux réunions importantes et on m'a donné des conseils régulièrement.

Enfin, ayant parlé avec d'autres stagiaires et après mes propres expériences, je peux affirmer que la qualité du stage dépend du responsable de la formation.

*stagiaire = person doing work experience

Questions

(a) How does Michel describe work experience? Complete the following sentence.   **2**

It is a way of _____

and _____ .

(b) Why it is not always easy to find a good work placement? State any **two** things.   **2**

_____

_____

(c) What do those doing work experience sometimes find difficult?   **1**

_____

_____

MARKS | DO NOT WRITE IN THIS MARGIN

Text 3 Questions (continued)

(d) Michel goes on to describe his two work placements.

    (i) As well as being exhausting, what does Michel say about his first placement? State **two** things.

      2

_____

_____

    (ii) What made Michel's second placement a positive experience? State any **two** things.

      2

_____

_____

(e) What is Michel's overall opinion of work experience?   Tick (✓) the correct statement.

    1

It is a waste of time and you are not paid any money.	
It is the only way of getting a job abroad.	
It can be a positive experience but it depends on the company.	

[END OF QUESTION PAPER]

MARKS DO NOT WRITE IN THIS MARGIN

ADDITIONAL SPACE FOR ANSWERS

MARKS DO NOT WRITE IN THIS MARGIN

ADDITIONAL SPACE FOR ANSWERS

[BLANK PAGE]

DO NOT WRITE ON THIS PAGE

FOR OFFICIAL USE

N5

National Qualifications 2016

Mark

X730/75/02

French Writing

MONDAY, 16 MAY

1:00 PM — 2:30 PM

Fill in these boxes and read what is printed below.

Full name of centre

Town

Forename(s)

Surname

Number of seat

Date of birth

Day   Month   Year   Scottish candidate number

Total marks — 20

Write your answer clearly, in **French**, in the space provided in this booklet.

You may use a French dictionary.

Additional space for answers is provided at the end of this booklet.

Use **blue** or **black** ink.

There is a separate question and answer booklet for Reading. You must complete your answers for Reading in the question and answer booklet for Reading.

Before leaving the examination room you must give both booklets to the Invigilator; if you do not, you may lose all the marks for this paper.

Total marks — 20

You are preparing an application for the job advertised below and you write an e-mail in **French** to the company.

Employeur: Chocolaterie 'Les délices charentaises'

Titre du Poste: Vendeur/vendeuse

Profil: Accueillir et conseiller les clients, aider à la caisse, ranger la boutique, savoir parler l'anglais et le français.

Renseignements: Pour plus de détails, contactez

Mme Laurent au courriel: chocolaterie.delicescharentaises@gmail.com

**Adresse: 38 rue du Château
18570 Graves Saint -Amant**

**Tél: 05 43 92 06 34
Fax: 05 43 92 06 35**

To help you to write your e-mail, you have been given the following checklist.
You must include **all** of these points

- Personal details (name, age, where you live)
- School/college/education experience until now
- Skills/interests you have which make you right for the job
- Related work experience
- The dates you would be available to work there
- Ask a question about the job.

Use all of the above to help you write the e-mail in **French**. The e-mail should be approximately 120—150 words. You may use a French dictionary.

MARKS | DO NOT WRITE IN THIS MARGIN

ANSWER SPACE

MARKS | DO NOT WRITE IN THIS MARGIN

ANSWER SPACE (continued)

MARKS | DO NOT WRITE IN THIS MARGIN

ANSWER SPACE (continued)

[Turn over

MARKS | DO NOT WRITE IN THIS MARGIN

ANSWER SPACE (continued)

[END OF QUESTION PAPER]

MARKS | DO NOT WRITE IN THIS MARGIN

ADDITIONAL SPACE FOR ANSWERS

Page seven

MARKS | DO NOT WRITE IN THIS MARGIN

ADDITIONAL SPACE FOR ANSWERS

N5

National Qualifications 2016

X730/75/03

Mark

French Listening

MONDAY, 16 MAY

2:50 PM — 3:20 PM (approx)

Fill in these boxes and read what is printed below.

Full name of centre

Town

Forename(s)

Surname

Number of seat

Date of birth

Day	Month	Year	Scottish candidate number

Total marks — 20

Attempt ALL questions.

You will hear two items in French. **Before you hear each item, you will have one minute to study the questions**. You will hear each item three times, with an interval of one minute between playings. You will then have time to answer the questions before hearing the next item.

You may NOT use a French dictionary.

Write your answers clearly, in **English**, in the spaces provided in this booklet. Additional space for answers is provided at the end of this booklet. If you use this space you must clearly identify the question number you are attempting.

Use **blue** or **black** ink.

You are not allowed to leave the examination room until the end of the test.

Before leaving the examination room you must give this booklet to the Invigilator; if you do not, you may lose all the marks for this paper.

MARKS | DO NOT WRITE IN THIS MARGIN

Total marks — 20

Attempt ALL questions

Item 1

Jean, a French student, speaks about a school exchange.

(a) When does Jean's school come to Scotland? State any **one** thing.

1

_____

_____

(b) Which personal details do pupils have to give their teachers before signing up for the exchange? State any **two** things.

2

_____

_____

(c) The pupils go to the Scottish school every morning. What other activities do they do:

  (i) in the afternoon? State any **two** things.

2

_____

_____

  (ii) in the evening with their host family? State any **one** thing.

1

_____

_____

(d) What did Jean particularly love about Scotland? State any **one** thing.

1

_____

_____

(e) What is the **main** benefit of taking part in a school exchange? Tick (✓) the correct statement.

1

It is a good way to get to know another country well	
You spend time away from home	
You have the opportunity to go away with your friends	

MARKS

Item 2

Jacques talks to Monique about her recent school exchange experience in Scotland.

(a) Why is Monique tired? State **two** things.   2

_____

_____

(b) Monique talks about the differences in the Scottish school.

    (i) What does she say about the school facilities? State any **one** thing.   1

_____

_____

    (ii) Why does she think Scottish pupils are lucky? State any **two** things.   2

_____

_____

(c) Monique took part in lessons in Scotland.

    (i) What happened in the history class? State any **one** thing.   1

_____

_____

    (ii) Why did she really enjoy the Spanish class? State **two** things.   2

_____

_____

(d) What did she not like about the school? State any **two** things.   2

_____

_____

[**Turn over**

MARKS | DO NOT WRITE IN THIS MARGIN

Item 2 (continued)

(e) What does Monique say about school uniform? Tick (✓) the two correct statements.

2

It is smart	
It is not expensive	
The pupils feel proud when they wear it	
It is not popular with the pupils	

[END OF QUESTION PAPER]

MARKS

DO NOT
WRITE IN
THIS
MARGIN

ADDITIONAL SPACE FOR ANSWERS

Page five

ADDITIONAL SPACE FOR ANSWERS

MARKS | DO NOT WRITE IN THIS MARGIN

National Qualifications 2016

X730/75/13

**French
Listening Transcript**

MONDAY, 16 MAY

2:50 PM — 3:20 PM (approx)

This paper must not be seen by any candidate.

The material overleaf is provided for use in an emergency only (eg the recording or equipment proving faulty) or where permission has been given in advance by SQA for the material to be read to candidates with additional support needs. The material must be read exactly as printed.

Instructions to reader(s)

For each item, read the English **once**, then read the French **three times**, with an interval of 1 minute between the three readings. On completion of the third reading, pause for the length of time indicated in brackets after the item, to allow the candidates to write their answers.

Where special arrangements have been agreed in advance to allow the reading of the material, those sections marked **(f)** should be read by a female speaker and those marked **(m)** by a male; those sections marked **(t)** should be read by the teacher.

(t)   Item Number One

Jean, a French student, speaks about a school exchange.

You now have one minute to study the questions for Item Number One.

(m)   Bonjour, je m'appelle Jean. Je vais vous parler de l'échange scolaire dans mon école. Tous les ans, nous passons une semaine au printemps en Ecosse.

Avant le séjour, chaque élève donne quelques détails personnels aux professeurs. Par exemple, des informations sur ses passe-temps, ses animaux domestiques, et s'il y a des choses qu'on n'aime pas manger. Ensuite, les profs essaient de mettre ensemble les élèves écossais et les élèves français qui partagent les mêmes intérêts.

A l'étranger, on loge chez son correspondant. Les journées sont très chargées. On passe les matinées en cours au collège. L'après-midi on va au parc d'attractions, on achète des cadeaux pour des amis ou on fait un tour de la ville. Le soir on reste en famille où on a l'occasion de goûter des spécialités du pays et on discute des événements de la journée.

J'ai vraiment adoré mon séjour en Ecosse. Les gens étaient vraiment chaleureux et le paysage était impressionnant. J'espère y retourner très bientôt. Je recommanderais un échange à tout le monde.

(2 minutes)

(t)   **Item Number Two**

Jacques talks to Monique about her recent school exchange experience in Scotland.

You now have one minute to study the questions for Item Number Two.

(m)   Salut Monique, tu es bien rentrée de ton échange scolaire?

(f)   Ça va merci mais je suis toujours un peu fatiguée après le voyage de vingt-quatre heures en car. En plus, on était vraiment occupé en Ecosse tous les jours.

(m)   Est-ce que tu as remarqué des différences au collège écossais?

(f)   Ben, oui. Il y avait beaucoup de différences. Par exemple, le bâtiment était bien équipé avec un grand terrain de sport. De plus les élèves écossais ont de la chance! Ils finissent les cours avant 16 heures, ils ont moins de devoirs et ils peuvent participer aux activités après l'école.

(m)   Est-ce que tu as participé aux cours?

(f)   Oui tous les jours. Par exemple en histoire il y avait un débat animé et on a fait des sondages. La leçon que j'ai aimée le plus était l'espagnol car le prof était passionné par sa matière et expliquait bien ses cours.

(m)   Est ce qu'il y avait des choses que tu n'aimais pas?

(f)   Ce que j'ai trouvé moins bien était que la pause-déjeuner était trop courte; la plupart des élèves avait juste le temps de prendre un sandwich. De plus il n'y avait pas beaucoup de choix à la cantine et les repas n'étaient pas équilibrés.

(m)   Et que penses-tu de l'uniforme scolaire?

(f)   Tiens, ça fait un look très habillé. C'est une bonne idée de s'habiller différemment pour travailler au collège. A mon avis, les élèves sont fiers de porter leur uniforme et de faire partie d'une communauté.

(m)   Ça a l'air très intéressant; je vais peut-être y aller l'année prochaine.

(2 minutes)

(t)   **End of test.**

Now look over your answers.

[END OF TRANSCRIPT]

[BLANK PAGE]

DO NOT WRITE ON THIS PAGE

NATIONAL 5

2017

N5

National Qualifications 2017

X730/75/01

Mark ▢

French Reading

MONDAY, 15 MAY

1:00 PM — 2:30 PM

Fill in these boxes and read what is printed below.

Full name of centre

Town

Forename(s)

Surname

Number of seat

Date of birth

Day	Month	Year	Scottish candidate number

Total marks — 30

Attempt ALL questions.

Write your answers clearly, in **English**, in the spaces provided in this booklet.

You may use a French dictionary.

Additional space for answers is provided at the end of this booklet. If you use this space you must clearly identify the question number you are attempting.

Use **blue** or **black** ink.

There is a separate question and answer booklet for Writing. You must complete your answer for Writing in the question and answer booklet for Writing.

Before leaving the examination room you must give both booklets to the Invigilator; if you do not, you may lose all the marks for this paper.

Total marks — 30

Attempt ALL questions

Text 1

Whilst in France, you read an article for school pupils about group work.

Le travail en groupe

Savoir travailler en équipe est essentiel dans la vie professionnelle ainsi que la vie de tous les jours. Il est donc indispensable d'acquérir les compétences pour pouvoir travailler en groupe à l'école et voici quelques conseils pour bien s'organiser.

Comment former un bon groupe.

Il est important de choisir des camarades de classe avec une variété de compétences et de trouver des personnes motivées qui veulent travailler. Mais attention: se mettre en groupe avec ses meilleurs amis n'est pas toujours une bonne idée. On risque de ne rien faire car on passe le temps à bavarder ou à rigoler.

Comment éviter le conflit.

Les disputes sont parfois inévitables. Pour bien s'entendre il faut rester respectueux envers les autres, écouter les opinions de tout le monde et apprendre à faire des compromis.

Comment travailler d'une manière efficace.

Tout d'abord il faut diviser les tâches équitablement et chaque membre du groupe doit avoir un rôle spécifique. Pour avoir de bons résultats tout le monde doit faire de son mieux et rester positif.

Questions

(a) Team work is important. Complete the sentence. **1**

Knowing how to work in a team is essential in your job as well as in

_____ .

MARKS | DO NOT WRITE IN THIS MARGIN

Text 1 Questions (continued)

(b) The article gives advice on forming a good group.

(i) What is it important to do? State any **two** things.   2

_____

_____

(ii) Why is it not always a good idea to go into a group with friends? State any **two** things.   2

_____

_____

(c) Arguments are sometimes inevitable. What can you do to avoid these? State any **two** things.   2

_____

_____

(d) The article goes on to discuss how to work effectively together. Give any **three** examples.   3

_____

_____

_____

[**Turn over**

MARKS | DO NOT WRITE IN THIS MARGIN

Text 2

Later, you read an article about heatwaves.

En France il est normal d'avoir du beau temps en été mais on parle de *canicule lorsqu'il fait extrêmement chaud. On peut dire qu'il y a une canicule quand les températures montent vite et la chaleur ne faiblit pas pendant soixante-douze heures.

Malheureusement les canicules arrivent de plus en plus. En 2003 la canicule a causé la mort de beaucoup de gens en France. Ce drame a fait scandale car le gouvernement a été accusé de ne pas avoir informé les Français des risques liés à la canicule.

Il est nécessaire d'aider les personnes qui souffrent de la chaleur, en particulier les personnes âgées et les jeunes enfants. Pour ne pas souffrir pendant la canicule il est recommandé de boire au moins deux litres d'eau par jour, de se mouiller les cheveux régulièrement et de ne pas faire trop d'exercice physique.

Pendant la période de canicule il vaut mieux rester à l'intérieur aux heures les plus chaudes. Si vous devez sortir, mettez un chapeau pour vous protéger la tête, essayez de rester à l'ombre ou allez aux endroits climatisés. A la maison gardez les fenêtres fermées pendant la journée pour que la chaleur ne rentre pas.

*canicule – heatwave

Questions

(a) The article describes what a heatwave is. Complete the sentence.   2

   You can say there is a heatwave when temperatures increase

   _____ and the heat doesn't go down for

   _____ hours.

(b) What happened as a result of the heatwave in 2003?   1

   _____

   _____

MARKS | DO NOT WRITE IN THIS MARGIN

Text 2 Questions (continued)

(c) The French government received a lot of criticism. Why? **1**

_____

_____

(d) The article recommends what you should do to avoid suffering during a heatwave. State **three** things. **3**

_____

_____

_____

(e) The article gives further advice on how to cope during a heatwave.

    (i) What should you do if you have to go out? State any **two** things. **2**

_____

_____

    (ii) What should you do at home? State **one** thing. **1**

_____

_____

[Turn over

Text 3

You also read an article about an interesting website.

Le stage en entreprise

Il est bien connu qu'un stage en entreprise apporte des avantages. Par exemple on apprend à gérer son temps et à travailler en équipe. Cependant il est souvent difficile de trouver un stage convenable.

Pour aider les étudiants en France le gouvernement a lancé le site www.monstageenligne.fr. Cela permet aux étudiants de trouver plus facilement un stage qui pourrait être utile pour leur future carrière. Ce site est avantageux pour les employeurs aussi parce qu'ils peuvent offrir les stages aux étudiants qui s'intéressent vraiment à leurs entreprises.

Alors le site est un succès? Voici l'expérience de David.

Quand j'avais 16 ans je voulais bien devenir cuisinier. Malheureusement mes parents ne pouvaient pas m'aider à trouver un stage car ils ne connaissaient personne dans ce domaine. Mais au lycée, mon prof de français m'a parlé du site et j'ai pu trouver un stage dans un restaurant renommé.

Après ce stage au restaurant, j'ai décidé que cette carrière n'était pas pour moi. Je trouvais les heures trop longues et on est debout toute la journée. Par contre il y avait des aspects positifs. J'ai pu développer mes compétences dans le monde du travail, j'ai plus de confiance en moi et je me suis bien entendu avec mes collègues.

Questions

(a) What are the advantages of doing work experience? Complete the sentence.

1

You learn to _____ and to

work in a team.

MARKS | DO NOT WRITE IN THIS MARGIN

Text 3 Questions (continued)

(b) The French government has launched a website. How does it help:

   (i) students? State any **one** thing.   1

   _____

   _____

   (ii) employers? State **one** thing.   1

   _____

   _____

(c) David talks about his experience of using the site. What job did he want to do when he was 16?   1

   _____

   _____

(d) Why were his parents not able to help him?   1

   _____

   _____

(e) David talks about his work experience.

   (i) What decision did he come to after this work experience?   1

   _____

   _____

   (ii) What did he not like about the job? State **two** things.   2

   _____

   _____

   (iii) What were the positive aspects? State any **two** things.   2

   _____

   _____

[END OF QUESTION PAPER]

MARKS DO NOT WRITE IN THIS MARGIN

ADDITIONAL SPACE FOR ANSWERS

MARKS | DO NOT WRITE IN THIS MARGIN

ADDITIONAL SPACE FOR ANSWERS

Page nine

[BLANK PAGE]

DO NOT WRITE ON THIS PAGE

N5

National Qualifications 2017

Mark

X730/75/02

French Writing

MONDAY, 15 MAY

1:00 PM — 2:30 PM

Fill in these boxes and read what is printed below.

Full name of centre

Town

Forename(s)

Surname

Number of seat

Date of birth

Day   Month   Year

Scottish candidate number

Total marks — 20

Write your answer clearly, in **French**, in the space provided in this booklet.

You may use a French dictionary.

Additional space for answers is provided at the end of this booklet.

Use **blue** or **black** ink.

There is a separate question and answer booklet for Reading. You must complete your answers for Reading in the question and answer booklet for Reading.

Before leaving the examination room you must give both booklets to the Invigilator; if you do not, you may lose all the marks for this paper.

Total marks — 20

You are preparing an application for the job advertised below and you write an e-mail in **French** to the company.

Hôtel Debrienne
Toulouse centre

Cherche (h/f) RECEPTIONNISTE

Profil: Anglais et français courant, bonne présentation, expérience dans l'hôtellerie souhaitée

Veuillez contacter: brienne@hoteldebrienne.com

To help you to write your e-mail, you have been given the following checklist.

You must include **all** of these points:

- Personal details (name, age, where you live)
- School/college/education experience until now
- Skills/interests you have which make you right for the job
- Related work experience
- Information about your hobbies
- Ask any two questions about the job.

Use all of the above to help you write the e-mail in **French**. The e-mail should be approximately 120–150 words. You may use a French dictionary.

ANSWER SPACE

ANSWER SPACE (continued)

ANSWER SPACE (continued)

ANSWER SPACE (continued)

MARKS

[END OF QUESTION PAPER]

MARKS | DO NOT WRITE IN THIS MARGIN

ADDITIONAL SPACE FOR ANSWERS

MARKS | DO NOT WRITE IN THIS MARGIN

ADDITIONAL SPACE FOR ANSWERS

FOR OFFICIAL USE

N5

National Qualifications 2017

Mark

X730/75/03

French Listening

MONDAY, 15 MAY

2:50 PM — 3:20 PM (approx)

Fill in these boxes and read what is printed below.

Full name of centre

Town

Forename(s)

Surname

Number of seat

Date of birth

Day	Month	Year	Scottish candidate number

Total marks — 20

Attempt ALL questions.

You will hear two items in French. **Before you hear each item, you will have one minute to study the questions.** You will hear each item three times, with an interval of one minute between playings. You will then have time to answer the questions before hearing the next item.

You may NOT use a French dictionary.

Write your answers clearly, in **English**, in the spaces provided in this booklet. Additional space for answers is provided at the end of this booklet. If you use this space you must clearly identify the question number you are attempting.

Use **blue** or **black** ink.

You are not allowed to leave the examination room until the end of the test.

Before leaving the examination room you must give this booklet to the Invigilator; if you do not, you may lose all the marks for this paper.

Total marks — 20

Attempt ALL questions

Item 1

Audrey talks about her experience of sharing a flat.

(a) Audrey lives in a flat in Marseille.

    (i) Why does she like her flat? State any **one** thing.   **1**

    _____

    _____

    (ii) What are the disadvantages? State any **one** thing.   **1**

    _____

    _____

(b) Audrey decided she wanted to share her flat. What type of person did she want to live with? State any **two** things.   **2**

    _____

    _____

(c) Sophie became Audrey's flatmate.

    (i) After a few months they started to argue. What did they argue about? State any **two** things.   **2**

    _____

    _____

    (ii) They decided to talk to each other about their problems. Why are things better now? State any **two** things.   **2**

    _____

    _____

MARKS | DO NOT WRITE IN THIS MARGIN

Item 2

Nathalie speaks to Benoît about his weekend at his grandparents'.

(a) Where do Benoît's grandparents live? State any **one** thing.   1

_____

_____

(b) What does he say about their house? Tick (✓) the **two** correct statements.   2

	Tick (✓)
It has a very big garden	
It is an old house	
There are 3 bedrooms	
There is a motorway nearby	

(c) What is the village like? State any **two** things.   2

_____

_____

(d) He says he wasn't bored at his grandparents' house. What did he do with them:

(i) on Saturday? State any **two** things.   2

_____

_____

(ii) on Sunday? State any **two** things.   2

_____

_____

[Turn over

MARKS | DO NOT WRITE IN THIS MARGIN

Item 2 (continued)

(e) Benoît gets on well with his grandparents. How does he describe them? State any **two** things.

2

_____

_____

(f) Why did he have an argument with his grandfather when he was 18? State **one** thing.

1

_____

_____

[END OF QUESTION PAPER]

MARKS | DO NOT WRITE IN THIS MARGIN

ADDITIONAL SPACE FOR ANSWERS

MARKS | DO NOT WRITE IN THIS MARGIN

ADDITIONAL SPACE FOR ANSWERS

MONDAY, 15 MAY

2:50 PM – 3:20 PM (approx)

This paper must not be seen by any candidate.

The material overleaf is provided for use in an emergency only (eg the recording or equipment proving faulty) or where permission has been given in advance by SQA for the material to be read to candidates with additional support needs. The material must be read exactly as printed.

Instructions to reader(s):

For each item, read the English **once**, then read the French **three times**, with an interval of 1 minute between the three readings. On completion of the third reading, pause for the length of time indicated in brackets after the item, to allow the candidates to write their answers.

Where special arrangements have been agreed in advance to allow the reading of the material, those sections marked **(f)** should be read by a female speaker and those marked **(m)** by a male; those sections marked **(t)** should be read by the teacher.

(t)   Item Number One

Audrey talks about her experience of sharing a flat.

You now have one minute to study the questions for Item Number One.

(f)   J'habite un appartement à Marseille dans le sud de la France. J'aime bien mon appartement car il se trouve à 5 minutes de mon travail et il y a beaucoup de magasins à proximité. Le seul inconvénient est que mon appartement se trouve au 4ème étage et il n'y a pas d'ascenseur.

Il y a un an j'ai décidé de partager mon appartement car je n'aimais pas vivre seule. Je voulais vivre avec quelqu'un de mon âge, qui ne fume pas et qui a les mêmes intérêts que moi. J'ai donc passé une annonce dans le journal et après quelques entretiens j'ai trouvé Sophie.

Au début tout s'est très bien passé entre Sophie et moi. Mais après quelques mois on a commencé à se disputer de plus en plus. Sophie ne faisait pas de tâches ménagères, elle faisait trop de bruit et elle laissait toujours les lumières allumées.

Heureusement qu'on a décidé de se parler et de résoudre nos problèmes. Maintenant Sophie fait la vaisselle, elle invite ses amis seulement le week-end et elle essaie d'économiser l'électricité. On est à nouveau de très bonnes amies.

(2 minutes)

(t) Item Number Two

Nathalie speaks to Benoît about his weekend at his grandparents'.

You now have one minute to study the questions for Item Number Two.

(f) Bonjour Benoît, comment ça va?

(m) Salut Nathalie, je vais très bien merci. Je viens de passer un week-end chez mes grands-parents.

(f) Ils habitent où?

(m) Ils habitent un petit village près de Lyon.

(f) Elle est comment la maison?

(m) Super chouette. C'est une vieille maison avec une belle piscine. Ce que je n'aime pas c'est qu'il y a une autoroute juste à côté et on entend la circulation qui passe. Mais on s'y habitue.

(f) Et c'est comment le village?

(m) Bien, bien. C'est tranquille mais il y a un bon réseau de transport en commun et des bus réguliers pour aller en ville.

(f) Et tu ne t'es pas trop ennuyé?

(m) Pas du tout. Il faisait super beau. Samedi, on a passé la journée à se baigner dans la piscine et à bronzer et puis le soir on a fait un barbecue sur la terrasse. C'était vraiment sympa. Dimanche matin, mon grand-père et moi sommes allés à la pêche. A midi on a mangé au restaurant et plus tard on a fait une petite promenade aux alentours.

(f) Alors tu t'entends très bien avec tes grands-parents?

(m) Ah oui je m'entends très bien avec eux. Ils sont très jeunes d'esprit, très actifs pour leur âge et je peux leur parler de tout. J'ai de la chance de les avoir.

(f) C'est bien ça. Et vous ne vous êtes jamais disputés?

(m) Oui une fois quand j'avais 18 ans. Je venais de passer mon permis de conduire et j'ai pris la voiture de mon grand-père sans demander la permission. Mon grand-père était vraiment en colère mais je me suis excusé et maintenant on en rigole.

(f) Il a l'air cool ton grand-père. J'aimerais bien le rencontrer un jour.

(m) La prochaine fois que je vais chez eux, viens avec moi, si tu veux.

(f) Merci ça serait sympa.

(2 minutes)

(t) End of test.

Now look over your answers.

[END OF TRANSCRIPT]

[BLANK PAGE]

DO NOT WRITE ON THIS PAGE

NATIONAL 5

2018

N5

National Qualifications 2018

Mark

X830/75/01

French Reading

THURSDAY, 17 MAY

1:00 PM — 2:30 PM

Fill in these boxes and read what is printed below.

Full name of centre

Town

Forename(s)

Surname

Number of seat

Date of birth

Day	Month	Year	Scottish candidate number

Total marks — 30

Attempt ALL questions.

Write your answers clearly, in **English**, in the spaces provided in this booklet.

You may use a French dictionary.

Additional space for answers is provided at the end of this booklet. If you use this space you must clearly identify the question number you are attempting.

Use **blue** or **black** ink.

There is a separate question and answer booklet for Writing. You must complete your answer for Writing in the question and answer booklet for Writing.

Before leaving the examination room you must give both booklets to the Invigilator; if you do not, you may lose all the marks for this paper.

Total marks — 30

Attempt ALL questions

Text 1

You read an item about an organisation called le Secours populaire, which helps children in France who are unable to go on a holiday.

LES VACANCES SONT POUR TOUT LE MONDE

Chaque année, le Secours populaire offre des vacances à des milliers d'enfants et voilà pourquoi. En France, plus de trente pour cent des enfants ne peuvent pas partir en vacances parce que ses parents n'ont pas les moyens. Néanmoins, aller en vacances, c'est important pour le bien-être de chacun. Cela permet d'oublier la routine quotidienne et on a la possibilité de se détendre.  Pourtant, ce que les jeunes aiment le plus c'est l'occasion de découvrir d'autres régions de la France et de se faire des copains.

Le Secours populaire organise aussi une journée spéciale à Paris au mois d'août pour tous les enfants qui n'ont pas pu partir en vacances. Les jeunes participent à une chasse aux trésors le matin, partagent un pique-nique géant à midi, et, pour terminer, ils assistent à un grand spectacle donné par des artistes célèbres.

Le Secours populaire rend plusieurs services aux familles pendant toute l'année. Par exemple, l'association aide les familles à se nourrir, à se soigner et à trouver un logement. Cette aide est possible grâce aux bénévoles qui travaillent pour l'association et aux gens qui lui donnent de l'argent.

Questions

(a) Some children are unable to go on holiday in France. What statistic supports this? Complete the sentence. **1**

_____ of children cannot go away on holiday.

MARKS | DO NOT WRITE IN THIS MARGIN

Text 1 questions (continued)

(b) Going on holiday is important. Why? Give any **two** reasons.

2

_____

_____

(c) What do young people like most about going on holiday? State any **one** thing.

1

_____

_____

(d) What activities take place during the special fun day in August? State any **two**.

2

_____

_____

_____

(e) The organisation helps families all year round.

   (i) What examples are there of this? State any **two**.

2

_____

_____

   (ii) What makes it possible to offer this help? State **two** things.

2

_____

_____

[Turn over

MARKS | DO NOT WRITE IN THIS MARGIN

Text 2

Leila posts her blog about going back to school after the holidays.

C'est la veille de *la rentrée scolaire et je suis un peu inquiète pour plusieurs raisons. J'ai des examens importants à passer à la fin de l'année scolaire, ma meilleure copine a déménagé et je ne m'entends pas bien avec certains profs.

L'année dernière c'était affreux en cours de maths parce que le prof était trop ennuyeux. Par conséquent il y avait beaucoup d'élèves qui ne s'intéressaient pas à ses cours. Ces élèves parlaient sans cesse et quelquefois ils lançaient des avions en papier. Enfin, c'était une perte de temps. Moi, j'ai décidé de faire des études supplémentaires chez moi et j'ai persuadé mon frère aîné de m'aider à faire des progrès.

Par contre, j'ai un très bon souvenir des cours d'histoire. A mon avis M. Duval était un bon prof car il était passionné par sa matière et il savait bien expliquer les choses. Quant à la discipline il imposait des règles mais il restait abordable en même temps et il ne criait jamais. Je dirais que M. Duval nous traitait comme des adultes car il nous encourageait à réfléchir et il écoutait nos opinions.

*la rentrée scolaire — going back to school after the summer holidays

Questions

(a) Why is Leila worried about going back to school? Give any **two** reasons.   2

_____

_____

(b) She talks about her maths class last year. What does she say about:

   (i) her maths teacher?   1

_____

   (ii) the pupils in the maths class? State any **two** things.   2

_____

_____

MARKS

Text 2 questions (continued)

(c) What did Leila decide to do? Tick (✓) the correct statement.   1

	Tick (✓)
She gave up maths.	
She spoke to another teacher.	
She did extra work at home.	

(d) Leila talks about her history teacher, M. Duval. Why was he a good teacher in her opinion? State any **one** thing.   1

_____

_____

(e) In what ways did he manage discipline in class? State any **two** things.   2

_____

_____

(f) M. Duval also treated his pupils as adults. What did he do? State any **one** thing.   1

_____

_____

[Turn over

Text 3

You read about the new trend of repair cafés.

Que peut-on faire avec des meubles cassés, des appareils qui ne marchent plus ou des vêtements déchirés? Ne les jette pas, répare-les au repair café!

Le concept du repair café a ses origines aux Pays-Bas et devient de plus en plus populaire en France. Alors c'est quoi un repair café?

Ce n'est pas un café comme les autres. On peut y apporter ses objets en mauvais état. Il y a des outils et matériels disponibles et on se met au travail avec le soutien d'un expert. Et voilà — un objet comme neuf!

Marco, 23 ans parle de son expérience au repair café.

«Je vais au repair café une fois par mois. A mon avis c'est une très bonne idée. De nos jours on jette énormément de choses qui sont encore utilisables. Le repair café apprend aux gens à penser autrement et encourage un changement de comportement. Ce genre de café est un premier pas vers une société durable.

Et d'un autre côté j'aime bien y aller car on rencontre de nouvelles personnes dans une ambiance décontractée.»

Questions

(a) What kind of things can you take to a repair café? State any **two** things.   2

_____

_____

(b) The article talks about where repair cafés started. Complete the sentence.   1

The repair café has its origins in _____ .

(c) The repair café is different from other cafés. In what ways? State any **two** things.   2

_____

_____

MARKS | DO NOT WRITE IN THIS MARGIN

Text 3 questions (continued)

(d) Marco goes to the repair café once a month.

    (i) Why does he think the café is a good idea? State any **three** things.   3

        _____

        _____

        _____

    (ii) What else does he like about it? State **two** things.   2

        _____

        _____

[END OF QUESTION PAPER]

ADDITIONAL SPACE FOR ANSWERS

MARKS DO NOT WRITE IN THIS MARGIN

MARKS

DO NOT
WRITE IN
THIS
MARGIN

ADDITIONAL SPACE FOR ANSWERS

[BLANK PAGE]

DO NOT WRITE ON THIS PAGE

N5

National Qualifications 2018

Mark ☐

X830/75/02

French Writing

THURSDAY, 17 MAY
1:00 PM — 2:30 PM

Fill in these boxes and read what is printed below.

Full name of centre

☐

Town

☐

Forename(s)

☐

Surname

☐

Number of seat

☐

Date of birth

Day	Month	Year	Scottish candidate number
☐☐	☐☐	☐☐	☐☐☐☐☐☐☐☐☐☐

Total marks — 20

Write your answer clearly, in **French**, in the space provided in this booklet.

You may use a French dictionary.

Additional space for answers is provided at the end of this booklet.

Use **blue** or **black** ink.

There is a separate question and answer booklet for Reading. You must complete your answers for Reading in the question and answer booklet for Reading.

Before leaving the examination room you must give both booklets to the Invigilator; if you do not, you may lose all the marks for this paper.

MARKS

Total marks — 20

You are preparing an application for the job advertised below and you write an e-mail in **French** to the company.

DISNEYLAND PARIS — Île-de-France

Vendeurs/Vendeuses Boutiques

Type d'emploi: Temps partiel

Profil : connaissance d'anglais et de français est essentielle

Veuillez envoyer CV + lettre de motivation à mlacroix@disneylandparis.fr

---

To help you to write your e-mail, you have been given the following checklist.

You must include **all** of these points:

- Personal details (name, age, where you live)
- School/college/education experience until now
- Skills/interests you have which make you right for the job
- Related work experience
- Your experience of working with people
- Why you would like to work in France

Use all of the above to help you write the e-mail in **French**. The e-mail should be approximately 120—150 words. You may use a French dictionary.

ANSWER SPACE

ANSWER SPACE (continued)

MARKS | DO NOT WRITE IN THIS MARGIN

ANSWER SPACE (continued)

MARKS DO NOT WRITE IN THIS MARGIN

ANSWER SPACE (continued)

[END OF QUESTION PAPER]

MARKS DO NOT WRITE IN THIS MARGIN

ADDITIONAL SPACE FOR ANSWERS

ADDITIONAL SPACE FOR ANSWERS

N5

National Qualifications 2018

Mark

X830/75/03

French Listening

THURSDAY, 17 MAY

2:50 PM — 3:20 PM (approx)

Fill in these boxes and read what is printed below.

Full name of centre

Town

Forename(s)

Surname

Number of seat

Date of birth

Day   Month   Year   Scottish candidate number

Total marks — 20

Attempt ALL questions.

You will hear two items in French. **Before you hear each item, you will have one minute to study the questions.** You will hear each item three times, with an interval of one minute between playings. You will then have time to answer the questions before hearing the next item.

You may NOT use a French dictionary.

Write your answers clearly, in **English**, in the spaces provided in this booklet. Additional space for answers is provided at the end of this booklet. If you use this space you must clearly identify the question number you are attempting.

Use **blue** or **black** ink.

You are not allowed to leave the examination room until the end of the test.

Before leaving the examination room you must give this booklet to the Invigilator; if you do not, you may lose all the marks for this paper.

MARKS | DO NOT WRITE IN THIS MARGIN

Total marks — 20

Attempt ALL questions

Item 1

Nathalie speaks about her experience of working abroad.

(a) When did Nathalie decide to go to England? State any **one** thing.   1

_____

_____

(b) Why did she go to Manchester? State any **one** thing.   1

_____

_____

(c) Her first job was in a bar. What did she not like about this job? State any **one** thing.   1

_____

(d) She says she loves her teaching job. State any **two** reasons she gives.   2

_____

_____

(e) What does she miss about France? State any **one** thing.   1

_____

_____

(f) Why does she say working abroad has been a positive experience for her? State any **two** things.   2

_____

_____

MARKS | DO NOT WRITE IN THIS MARGIN

Item 2

Paula speaks to Yannick about his recent interview for a part-time job.

(a) Where did the interview take place?

    1

_____

(b) He says he did well in the interview but the day started badly. What happened to him? Tick (✓) the **two** correct statements.

    2

	Tick (✓)
He spilled coffee over his shirt	
His car wouldn't start	
He couldn't find his keys	
The bus was late	

(c) The first question was about his personal qualities. What qualities did he say he has? State any **two** things.

    2

_____

_____

(d) What else did they ask him about? State any **two** things.

    2

_____

_____

(e) What will his tasks be if he gets the job? State any **two** things.

    2

_____

_____

(f) How many hours will he work a week?

    1

_____

_____

(g) What would he like to do with the money he earns? State any **two** things.

    2

_____

_____

[END OF QUESTION PAPER]

ADDITIONAL SPACE FOR ANSWERS

ADDITIONAL SPACE FOR ANSWERS

MARKS | DO NOT WRITE IN THIS MARGIN

[BLANK PAGE]

DO NOT WRITE ON THIS PAGE

National Qualifications 2018

X830/75/13

French
Listening Transcript

THURSDAY, 17 MAY

2:50 PM – 3:20 PM (approx)

This paper must not be seen by any candidate.

The material overleaf is provided for use in an emergency only (eg the recording or equipment proving faulty) or where permission has been given in advance by SQA for the material to be read to candidates with additional support needs. The material must be read exactly as printed.

Instructions to reader(s):

For each item, read the English **once**, then read the French **three times**, with an interval of 1 minute between the three readings. On completion of the third reading, pause for the length of time indicated in brackets after the item, to allow the candidates to write their answers.

Where special arrangements have been agreed in advance to allow the reading of the material, those sections marked **(f)** should be read by a female speaker and those marked **(m)** by a male; those sections marked **(t)** should be read by the teacher.

(t) Item number one.

Nathalie speaks about her experience of working abroad.

You now have one minute to study the questions for item number one.

(f) Aujourd'hui je vais vous parler de mon expérience de travail à l'étranger. Quand j'avais 21 ans, après mes études en France, j'ai décidé d'aller en Angleterre pour trouver du travail. Je suis allée à Manchester car j'y avais de la famille et je connaissais bien la ville. J'ai trouvé du travail dans un bar au centre-ville. Je n'aimais pas trop ce travail car je devais travailler de très longues heures et le patron était trop sévère.

J'ai décidé de quitter ce boulot et maintenant j'ai la chance d'avoir un poste comme professeur de français à l'université de Manchester. J'adore ce travail: c'est très bien payé, les horaires sont flexibles et j'ai un bon rapport avec les étudiants.

La France me manque un petit peu surtout le climat et la cuisine, mais je suis très heureuse ici. Pour moi, travailler à l'étranger est une expérience très positive. Je parle anglais couramment, j'ai découvert une autre culture que la mienne et j'ai fait la connaissance de beaucoup de gens très différents.

(2 minutes)

(t) Item number two

Paula speaks to Yannick about his recent interview for a part-time job.

You now have one minute to study the questions for item number two.

(f) Bonjour Yannick, ça va?

(m) Oui je viens de passer un entretien dans un salon de coiffure.

(f) Alors comment ça s'est passé ?

(m) Ça va je crois. Mais la journée a mal commencé. D'abord mon réveil n'a pas sonné ce matin, ensuite j'ai renversé du café sur ma chemise, alors il a fallu que je me change, et finalement le bus avait du retard. Heureusement je suis arrivé juste à l'heure.

(f) Est-ce qu'ils ont posé beaucoup de questions?

(m) Oui pas mal. La première question était sur mes qualités. Alors j'ai répondu que je suis toujours très poli, que j'aime travailler avec le public et qu'on peut toujours compter sur moi.

(f) C'est une bonne réponse ça. Ils ont posé quoi d'autre comme questions ?

(m) Ben! Les choses habituelles comme pourquoi je veux le travail, quels sont mes loisirs préférés et aussi ce que je veux faire à l'avenir. Je crois que j'ai assez bien répondu.

(f) Et c'est quoi comme travail exactement ?

(m) Un peu de tout. Je devrai répondre au téléphone, prendre les réservations et laver les cheveux des clients.

(f) Combien d'heures travailleras-tu ?

(m) Comme c'est à mi-temps, je travaillerai chaque mercredi et samedi — en tout 15 heures par semaine. Je gagnerai 11 euros de l'heure.

(f) Qu'est-ce que tu voudrais faire avec cet argent ?

(m) Ben! j'aimerais me payer les sorties, m'acheter des vêtements et s'il m'en reste je voudrais économiser un peu.

(f) Ecoute je te souhaite bonne chance et n'oublie pas de m'envoyer un SMS dès que tu auras des nouvelles.

(m) D'accord

(2 minutes)

(t) End of test.

Now look over your answers.

[END OF TRANSCRIPT]

[BLANK PAGE]

DO NOT WRITE ON THIS PAGE

NATIONAL 5

Answers

NATIONAL 5 FRENCH 2016

Reading

Text 1

(a) Thirteen/13 **year**(s)

(b) (i) • Sand castle (building)**competition**(s)/**contest**(s)
    • (Fly) kite(s)/kite flying

  (ii) *Any one from:*
    • *Relaxing* **in the sun**
    • Reading/read (a book)

(c) Those/people who don't want to miss the **sporting events**/people who (want to/enjoy/rather) watch/see **sporting events** (in the summer)
People who enjoy sporting events

(d) • (Lots/many of them) don't have the **chance/ possibility/opportunity** to go/**can't** go to the sea(side)/beach
   or
   Gives them/they have the **possibility** to/ **opportunity/chance to** go/they **can** go to the beach

  • (They can go) **without leaving/don't need to leave** Paris

(e) *Any one from:*
  • *(Great/good) meeting place/point/spot for him and his* **friends**/he can hang out with his **friends**
  • It is/was free/he (and his friends)/me (and my friends) can go there for free/they don't have to pay/it doesn't cost.

(f) (i) **Not allowed to/not possible to/do not have the right to/can't** swim/bathe/go bathing there

  (ii) *Any one from:*
    • Go to a **sea**(side) resort/the sea(side)
    • Go to an **outdoor** pool/pool **in the fresh/open air**

Text 2

(a) • Spend/pass (more) time **outdoors/outside**
   Like to be outdoors
  • To feel/it is safe(r)/(more) secure/has a sense of security

(b) She was bored
(Second box ticked)

(c) • That no one knew her/people didn't know her/she knew no one/didn't know anyone
  • A **choice/selection** of entertainment/**a lot of/plenty of/various** things to do

(d) *Any one from:*
  • The traffic began/started to **annoy/irritate her/get on her nerves**/the traffic **is annoying/irritated her/ annoyed her**
  • **She** was (always) rushed/in a rush/hurry (everyday)

(e) • (Two) dogs (love) **running** in the field(s)/the countryside
  • **Forget** the worries/concerns/problems of **every day/daily** life/she doesn't have to worry about **everyday** life/leaves her **daily** worries behind

(f) • (Take advantage of/benefit from) the bustling **city/ town life**/the busyness/the liveliness of the **city/ town**
  • Quiet/peaceful (life) **in the country(side)**/ tranquillity of **the country(side)**

Text 3

(a) • Having/getting **practical/hands on/useful/helpful/ right** experience
  • Earning/gaining/making/(a little/a bit of) money

(b) *Any two from:*
  • (One in two chance of a placement) being a waste of time/it can be a waste of time
  • (In some/certain companies you have/there are) **too many/much/lots of** responsibilities
  • (In other/some companies) you (only/just) serve/ make coffee

(c) Managing/doing/handling **new** tasks/du**ti**es

(d) (i) • **The boss/manager** was (always) in a bad mood
    • He was **scared/frightened/afraid/found it difficult/struggled** to ask questions (if he had a problem)

  (ii) *Any two from:*
    • He learned lots/an enormous/tremendous amount (of things)/he was taught a lot
    • He attended/went to (important) meetings
    • He was given/they gave him advice (regularly)

(e) It can be a positive experience but it depends on the company
(Third box ticked)

Writing

Candidates will write a piece of extended writing in the modern language by addressing six bullet points. These bullet points will follow on from a job-related scenario. The bullet points will cover the four contexts of society, learning, employability and culture, to allow candidates to use and adapt learned material. The first four bullet points will be the same each year and the last two will change to suit the scenario. Candidates need to address these "unpredictable bullet points" in detail to access the full range of marks.

Category	Mark	Content	Accuracy	Language resource — variety, range, structures
Very good	**20**	The job advert has been addressed in a full and balanced way. The candidate uses detailed language. The candidate addresses the advert completely and competently, including **information in response to both unpredictable bullet points.** A range of verbs/verb forms, tenses and constructions is used. Overall this comes over as a competent, well-thought-out and serious application for the job.	The candidate handles all aspects of grammar and spelling accurately, although the language may contain one or two minor errors. Where the candidate attempts to use language more appropriate to Higher, a slightly higher number of inaccuracies need not detract from the overall very good impression.	The candidate is comfortable with the first person of the verb and generally uses a different verb in each sentence. Some modal verbs and infinitives may be used. There is good use of adjectives, adverbs and prepositional phrases and, where appropriate, word order. There may be a range of tenses. The candidate uses co-ordinating conjunctions and/or subordinate clauses where appropriate. The language of the e-mail flows well.
Good	**16**	The job advert has been addressed competently. There is less evidence of detailed language. The candidate uses a reasonable range of verbs/verb forms. Overall, the candidate has produced a genuine, reasonably accurate attempt at applying for the specific job, **even though he/she may not address one of the unpredictable bullet points.**	The candidate handles a range of verbs fairly accurately. There are some errors in spelling, adjective endings and, where relevant, case endings. Use of accents is less secure, where appropriate. Where the candidate is attempting to use more complex vocabulary and structures, these may be less successful, although basic structures are used accurately. There may be one or two examples of inaccurate dictionary use, especially in the unpredictable bullet points.	There may be repetition of verbs. There may be examples of listing, in particular when referring to school/college experience, without further amplification. There may be one or two examples of a co-ordinating conjunction, but most sentences are simple sentences. The candidate keeps to more basic vocabulary, particularly in response to either or both unpredictable bullet points.

Category	Mark	Content	Accuracy	Language resource — variety, range, structures
Satisfactory	**12**	The job advert has been addressed fairly competently. The candidate makes limited use of detailed language. The language is fairly repetitive and uses a limited range of verbs and fixed phrases, e.g. *I like, I go, I play*. The candidate copes fairly well with areas of personal details, education, skills, interests and work experience but does not deal fully with the two unpredictable bullet points **and indeed may not address either or both of the unpredictable bullet points.** On balance, however, the candidate has produced a satisfactory job application in the specific language.	The verbs are generally correct but may be repetitive. There are quite a few errors in other parts of speech — gender of nouns, cases, singular/plural confusion, for instance. Prepositions may be missing, e.g. *I go the town*. Overall, there is more correct than incorrect.	The candidate copes with the first and third person of a few verbs, where appropriate. A limited range of verbs is used. Sentences are basic and mainly brief. There is minimal use of adjectives, probably mainly after is e.g. *Chemistry is interesting*. The candidate has a weak knowledge of plurals. There may be several spelling errors, e.g. reversal of vowel combinations.
Unsatisfactory	**8**	The job advert has been addressed in an uneven manner and/or with insufficient use of detailed language. The language is repetitive, e.g. *I like, I go, I play* may feature several times. There may be little difference between Satisfactory and Unsatisfactory. **Either or both of the unpredictable bullet points may not have been addressed.** There may be one sentence which is not intelligible to a sympathetic native speaker.	Ability to form tenses is inconsistent. There are errors in many other parts of speech — gender of nouns, cases, singular/plural confusion, for instance. Several errors are serious, perhaps showing mother tongue interference. The detail in the unpredictable bullet points may be very weak. Overall, there is more incorrect than correct.	The candidate copes mainly only with the personal language required in bullet points 1 and 2. The verbs "is" and "study" may also be used correctly. Sentences are basic. An English word may appear in the writing. There may be an example of serious dictionary misuse.

Category	Mark	Content	Accuracy	Language resource — variety, range, structures
Poor	4	The candidate has had considerable difficulty in addressing the job advert. There is little evidence of the use of detailed language. Three or four sentences may not be understood by a sympathetic native speaker. **Either or both of the unpredictable bullet points may not have been addressed.**	Many of the verbs are incorrect. There are many errors in other parts of speech — personal pronouns, gender of nouns, cases, singular/plural confusion, prepositions, for instance. The language is probably inaccurate throughout the writing.	The candidate cannot cope with more than one or two basic verbs. The candidate displays almost no knowledge of the present tense of verbs. Verbs used more than once may be written differently on each occasion. Sentences are very short. The candidate has a very limited vocabulary. Several English words may appear in the writing. There are examples of serious dictionary misuse.
Very poor	0	The candidate is unable to address the job advert. **The two unpredictable bullet points may not have been addressed.** Very little is intelligible to a sympathetic native speaker.	Virtually nothing is correct.	The candidate may only cope with the verbs to have and to be. Very few words are written correctly in the modern language. English words are used. There may be several examples of mother tongue interference. There may be several examples of serious dictionary misuse.

Listening

Item 1

(a) *Any one from:*
- (In) spring
- Every year/(one week) every year/once a year

(b) *Any two from:*
- Their hobbies/interests/pastimes/things you like/are interested in
- Their animals/pets/animals in their house/household animals/domestic animals
- If there are things/foods/is anything they **don't** like eating/to eat/**can't** eat

(c) (i) *Any two from:*
- Go to a theme park/amusement park/fairground
- Buy/shop for/get **presents/gifts/souvenirs** (for friend(s))
- Visit/tour of the town/city, walk around the town/city/town tour(s)

(ii) *Any one from:*
Chance to
- Taste/try specialities **of the country/region/area/Scotland**, eat a traditional/special **Scottish** meal, **national** speciality foods
- Talk/discuss/speak/tell/chat about/share (the events of) the/his/her/their **day**/how the **day** went/what happened during the **day**

(d) *Any one from:*
- The people/locals/Scottish (people)/Scots
- Scenery/countryside/landscape/the views

(e) It is a good way to get know a country well
(First box ticked)

Item 2

(a) • **24 hour** (coach/bus) journey/ride/she was travelling for **24 hours**

or
Long coach/bus journey/ride

- She was (really) busy/(really) occupied/it was busy (in Scotland) (every day)/she did a lot (of activities) (when she was there)

(b) (i) *Any one from:*
- (The building/school/it was) well-equipped
- **Big/large sports** ground(s)/pitch(es)/(playing) field(s)/area(s)/space(s)

(ii) *Any two from:*
- Finish/school ends/finishes before/at/by 4pm/16.00
- **Less** homework/**not as much** homework
- (Can take part/participate in) activities/clubs/**at the end of the day/after school**/extra-curricular activities

(c) (i) *Any one from:*
- (Lively/animated) debate/argument/discussion
- Did survey(s)/questionnaire(s)

(ii) • Teacher was passionate/enthusiastic/excited (about subject) really likes/loves (the subject)
- Explained/explains well/explained/explains the lesson(s)/everything/it (well)/teacher was good at explaining

(d) *Any two from:*
- The lunch/dinner break is (too/very) short/not long (enough)/not as long/shorter
- **Just/only** (enough) **time** to eat a sandwich
- Not enough/not a lot of/not much/no choice in the canteen/there aren't many options in the canteen
- Meals/menu/food/canteen not balanced/unbalanced/not healthy

(e) • It's smart
- They feel proud
(First and third boxes ticked)

NATIONAL 5 FRENCH 2017

Reading

Text 1

(a) Everyday/daily/day to day life/life everyday.

(b) (i) • (Choose/pick/have) (classmate(s)/friend(s)/ people/pupil(s) with) different/a variety/mix of skill(s)/competence(s)/capabilitie(s)/knowledge
   • Find motivated people/person
   OR
   • People who are motivated to work/want to work/like working/work well.

   (ii) *Any two from:*
   • Do nothing/not doing anything/not on task/ don't get the work done/not working
   • Chat/talk/speak/gossip
   • Laugh (a lot/too much)/having a laugh/joke/ fun.

(c) *Any two from:*
   • (Be) respectful/respect others
   • Listen to (everyone's) opinion(s)/others
   • (Learn how to/make) compromise.

(d) *Any three from:*
   • Divide the task(s) equally/evenly
   • Everyone has a specific/different role/task/job/ specify roles
   • Do your best/one's/their best
   • Stay/remain/be positive.

Text 2

(a) • Quickly/quick/fast
   • 72/seventy two.

(b) Many/a lot of/numerous people died/death(s).

(c) Did not inform/tell/warn/give advice to (the French/ France) of/about the risk(s)/danger(s).

(d) *Any three from:*
   • Drink (at least/more than) two litres of water a/per day/don't drink less than 2 litres of water a/per day
   • Soak/wet/moisten your hair (regularly)
   • Don't do/avoid too much/many/a lot of (physical) exercise/sport
   • Stay in at the hottest time/hour(s).

(e) (i) *Any two from:*
   • Wear/put on a hat/cap
   OR
   • Protect/cover your head
   • Stay/rest in the shade/shadow(s)
   • Go to air conditioned place(s).

   (ii) Close/shut your windows/keep your windows closed/shut during the day/for the day/all the day.

Text 3

(a) Manage (one's/your) time.

(b) (i) *Any one from:*
   • To find a (work) placement/work experience/ training (course) (more) easily/easier
   • Useful/helps/helps prepare for their future career.

(ii) • They can offer work placements/training (course)/experience to students
   OR
   • They can find students who are interested/have an interest in their business/company/firm/ enterprise.

(c) Cook/chef.

(d) • Didn't know anyone/someone in this/that/the field/ job/line of work/area of work/domain
   OR
   • Didn't know any/a chef/cook.

(e) (i) Job/it/this/being a chef/this career wasn't for him/he didn't want to be a chef.

   (ii) • Long hours
   • On your feet/standing (up)/stood (up) all day/ the whole time/the whole day/all the day.

   (iii) *Any two from:*
   • Developed/gained skills/competences/ capabilities/abilities/knowledge (in the world of work)
   • Became/has become confident/increased in/ gained in/improved/developed/gave him confidence
   OR
   • He is more confident/he has more confidence
   • Got/gets on well with colleagues/likes working with his colleagues.

Writing

Please see the assessment criteria for Writing on pages 100–102.

Listening

Item 1

(a) (i) *Any one from:*
   • 5 minutes from (her) work/her job
   • A lot of/lots of/many shops
   OR
   • Shops near(by)/close/near the shops.

   (ii) *Any one from:*
   • On 4th floor/4th storey (accept any spelling)
   • No lift/elevator/she has to walk up (stairs).

(b) *Any two from:*
   • Same/similar age
   • Doesn't smoke/non-smoker/shouldn't smoke
   • Same/similar interests/likes same/similar things/ same things in common.

(c) (i) *Any two from:*
   • The housework/housekeeping/chores/cleaning/ tidying/helping around the house/flat
   • The noise she/Sophie made (a lot of/too much) noise/she was noisy/she was (too) loud/there was (a lot of/too much) noise
   • The light(s) left on/light(s) not turned off/ light(s) always on.

   (ii) *Any two from:*
   • Sophie/she does the washing-up/dishes
   • (She/they) (only) invite(s) friends/people at the weekend/friends come at the weekend
   • (She/they) save(s)/conserve(s)/economise(s)/ use(s) less/do(es) not waste/do(es) not use as much electricity/energy.

Item 2

(a) *Any one from:*
- A small/little village
- Near Lyon (accept any spelling).

(b) • It is an old house (box 2)
   • There is a motorway nearby (box 4).

(c) *Any two from:*
- It is quiet/peaceful/calm/tranquil (accept any spelling)
- There is (a lot of/loads of) (good) (public) transport
- Bus/coach goes/buses/coaches go to town/city (centre)
  OR
- Regular bus(es)/coach(es)/bus(es)/coach(es) come(s) regularly/there are many/a lot of buses/coaches.

(d) (i) *Any two from:*
- Swimming/going to/in (swimming) pool
- Sunbathing/tanning/tan
- (Had) a barbecue/BBQ (on terrace).

(ii) *Any two from:*
- Fishing/fish
- (Went to a) restaurant
  OR
- Went out to eat/out for lunch/out for dinner
- (Went for a) (small) walk/walked.

(e) *Any two from:*
- Young at heart/young spirited/youthful/act young
- (Very) active (for their age)
- He/You can talk/speak to them (about anything)
  They are good to talk/speak to/easy to talk to
  They can talk (to each other) about anything
- (He is) lucky to have them.

(f) Took/drove/used grandfather's/his/their car (without permission/asking).

NATIONAL 5 FRENCH 2018

Reading

Text 1

(a) <u>More than/Over</u> 30%/30 out of 100

(b) *Any two from:*
- Good for your well-being/health/good being
- Allows you to forget/get out of/gives you a break from your <u>daily/everyday routine/life</u>
- To relax/chill

(c) *Any one from:*
- To discover other parts/regions/areas of <u>France</u>
- Making friend<u>s</u>

(d) *Any two from:*
- (Taking part in) a/the treasure hunt(ing) <u>in the morning</u>
- (Sharing) a/the <u>giant/huge</u> picnic <u>at midday/ noon/12/lunch</u>
- (Attending) a/the <u>big show/concert</u> given by <u>famous/celebrity</u> artists/performers/with celebrities performing

(e) (i) *Any two from:*
- Gives them food/feeds them/helps families who need food/to feed themselves/to get food/ enough to eat/helps families to eat
- (It helps them) to look after/tend/take care of <u>themselves</u>
- Finds accommodation/lodging/housing/a place to stay/a flat/an apartment/a house/homes (for families)

(ii)
- Volunteers (working for them)/voluntary workers
- (People/the public) donating/giving <u>money</u>/ donations of <u>money/monetary/financial</u> donations

Text 2

(a) *Any two from:*
- Sitting <u>important</u> exams <u>at the end of the (school) year</u>
- <u>Best</u> friend has moved (away/house/school)
- Doesn't get on with <u>certain/some/particular</u> teachers

(b) (i) (He/she/they)was/were <u>too/very/really</u> boring

(ii) *Any two from:*
- Weren't interested <u>in the class/lesson(s)/ course</u>/didn't find <u>the class/lesson(s)/course</u> interesting
- They talked/spoke <u>non-stop/all the time/ constantly/always/continuously</u>
- (Sometimes) they <u>threw/launched</u> paper airplanes/planes of paper

(c) She did extra work at home

(d) *Any one from:*
- Passionate about/has a passion for/is keen about/ excited by <u>history</u>/his/the <u>subject</u>
- Knew how to explain (things) <u>well</u>/He was <u>good</u> at explaining

(e) *Any two from:*
- He <u>imposed/set/had/made</u> rules
- Remained/was approachable (at the same time)

- He <u>never</u> shouted/yelled/<u>didn't</u> shout/yell

(f) *Any one from:*
- Encouraged them <u>to think/reflect/</u>encouraged <u>reflection</u>
- Listened to (their/others') <u>opinions/views</u>

Text 3

(a) *Any two from:*
- <u>Broken/cracked</u> furniture
- Appliances/apparatus/devices <u>which no longer/ don't work/function</u>
- <u>Ripped/torn</u> clothes/clothes with holes

(b) The Netherlands/Holland

(c) *Any two from:*
- (One/you can) take/bring/(the café) accepts object(s) in a <u>poor/bad</u> state/condition/<u>broken</u> products
- Tools <u>and</u> materials/equipment/gear are available/ there
  NB: must write tools + one other to be awarded the mark
- <u>Work/get the job done with/get help/support from</u> an expert

(d) (i) *Any three from:*
- People <u>throw out/get rid of</u> (a lot of) things which are (still) <u>useful/usable/still function/ work/can be reused</u>
- (Teaches/getting) people to think <u>differently/ otherwise/another way</u>
- Encourages a change in <u>behaviour</u>
- (First) step towards a sustainable/lasting/ durable society

(ii)
- Meet/get to know/come across <u>new</u> people
- A relaxed/chilled/laid back atmosphere/ ambiance/environment

Writing

Please see the assessment criteria for Writing on pages 100–102.

Listening

Item 1

1. (a) *Any one from:*
- When <u>she was/aged</u> 21
- <u>After</u> her studies

(b) *Any one from:*
- (Had/has) family <u>there/in Manchester</u>
- Knew the town/city <u>well</u>/has <u>good</u> knowledge of the city

(c) *Any one from:*
- <u>Very</u> long hours/the hours were <u>too</u> long
- Boss was <u>too/very/really</u> strict/severe/harsh

(d) *Any two from:*
- (Very) well paid/(very) good/great/excellent/ brilliant pay
- Flexible <u>hours</u>
- <u>Gets on/along (well)/has a good rapport/ relationship with</u> students/learners/pupils

(e) *Any one from:*
- Weather/climate
- (French) food/cuisine/<u>the</u> cooking

(f) *Any two from:*
- Speaks **fluent** English/speaks English **fluently**
- **Discovered/got to know/experienced**/**learnt** a new/another/a different culture/way of life (other than her own)
- Met/got to know/knows **many**/**a lot** of (very) **different** people

Item 2

(a) Hairdresser's/hair(dressing) salon/barber's (salon/shop)

(b) • He spilled coffee over his shirt
- The bus was late

(c) *Any two from:*
- **Always/very/really** polite
- **Likes/enjoys** working with people/the public
- Someone you can (always) count/rely on

(d) *Any two from:*
- Why he wants **the** job/to work **there**/a job **there**
- What are his **favourite/preferred** leisure/free/spare time activities/hobbies/pastimes
  What are his **favourite/preferred** things to do in his free/spare time
- What he **wants** to do in the future/what he's **going to** do in the future

(e) *Any two from:*
- Answer/respond to the phone
- Take/make reservations/bookings/book (people in for) appointments
- Wash/clean hair

(f) 15

(g) *Any two from:*
- To go/going out/(a) night(s) out/outing(s)
- **Buy/get/spend it on** clothes
- **Save** (up) (a bit/some)